by James Stevenson

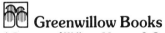 **Greenwillow Books**
A Division of William Morrow & Company, Inc.
New York

PRINTED IN THE UNITED STATES OF AMERICA   FIRST EDITION

1   2   3   4   5   6   7   8   9   10

LIBRARY OF CONGRESS CATALOGING IN PUBLICATION DATA
STEVENSON, JAMES (DATE)   MONTY.
SUMMARY: WHEN MONTY THE ALLIGATOR GOES ON VACATION, A RABBIT, DUCK, AND FROG LOOK FOR ANOTHER WAY TO CROSS THE RIVER TO SCHOOL.
[1. ALLIGATORS—FICTION.   2. ANIMALS—FICTION.   3. CARTOONS AND COMICS]
I. TITLE.   PZ7.S84748MO   [E]   78-11409
ISBN 0-688-80209-5   ISBN 0-688-84209-7 LIB. BDG.

FOR
S.

EVERY MORNING, ARTHUR AND DORIS AND TOM WALKED TO SCHOOL TOGETHER.
WHEN THEY CAME TO THE WIDE RIVER, THEY LOOKED FOR MONTY.

MONTY WAS ALWAYS ASLEEP, SNORING.
WAKE UP, MONTY! THIS IS A SCHOOL DAY!
GUG... GUGGLE.. GORGA...GUG...

THEY CLIMBED ON
MONTY'S BACK, AND
HE SWAM ACROSS
THE RIVER.

WHEN THEY GOT TO THE FAR SIDE,
DORIS AND ARTHUR AND TOM WENT
TO SCHOOL. MONTY WENT BACK
TO SLEEP.

...BUT MONTY
DID NOT COME.

THEN MONTY FLOATED BY.
MONTY! WHERE HAVE YOU BEEN?
I AM ON VACATION.
THIS IS NOT VACATION TIME!
IT IS FOR ME. THIS IS ALLIGATOR VACATION.

WELL, WHAT ARE
WE SUPPOSED
TO DO NOW?

IT BEATS
ME.

EVERYBODY
START
THINKING.

WHAT ARE YOU
THINKING, DORIS?

I'M THINKING
WE NEED A NEW
ALLIGATOR.

THAT'S NOT
THINKING.
THAT'S JUST
WISHING.

THEY WENT BACK TO SHORE, AND
PUT THEIR BOOKS IN THE SUN TO DRY.
TOM AND DORIS SAT DOWN.

HEY... I FOUND A BOARD!

THEY DECIDED TO TRY IT WITH DORIS BECAUSE SHE WAS THE LIGHTEST. DORIS STOOD ON THE BOARD.

BETTER,
BUT NOT PERFECT.

SPLASH

IT WAS CLEAR THAT THEY WOULD HAVE TO SWIM ACROSS.

WE THOUGHT YOU WERE ON VACATION...
I AM, BUT SOMETIMES WHEN I AM ON VACATION I TAKE A DAY OFF

THANKS FOR THE RIDE, MONTY!
IS THERE ANY CHANCE YOU'LL BE HERE THIS AFTERNOON, MONTY?
MONTY?
GUG... GUGGLE...
BUT MONTY HAD ALREADY STARTED TO SNORE.